# CONTENTS

Words in **bold** are explained in the glossary.

# Mike the pilot

I am an airline pilot.

Today I am flying from London to New York.

London is in England.

New York is in America.

It takes six hours to fly there.

# Let's look at the plane

I am going to fly this jumbo jet.

A jumbo jet is one of the biggest planes in the world.

Tail

Wing

Engine

Wheels

A jumbo jet has 188 windows and 18 wheels.

Cockpit

Windows

Door

I sit in the cockpit.

# Checking the plane

I get to the airport early.

First I check the outside
of the plane.

I check the wheels.

I check the lights.

I look in the engines.

It is important that
everything is working.

Wheels

# In the cockpit

I am the **captain**.

Don is the **co-pilot**.

I check that all the controls are working.

Controls

Then I check the weather forecast.

Sunny

Rainy

Stormy

Snowy

Don checks the map.

Map

# Take-off

We have done our checks.

We are ready for take-off.

We start the engines.

Runway

As the plane moves down the **runway**, it goes faster and faster.

Then it takes off into the sky.

Wheels

The wheels fold up into the plane.

# Flying to America

There are 412 passengers on this plane.

Soon the flight attendants will give them food and drinks.

Some of the passengers are watching a film.

Flight attendant

# Pilots at work

Don and I are working.

Don checks the weather and the fuel.

I check the plane's speed.

We are flying at 920 kilometres per hour.

**In-flight meal**

The flight attendant
brings us a meal in
the cockpit.

# Landing

We are getting near to New York.

I ask **air-traffic control** if
we can land.

Air-traffic control

They check the weather.

They check for other planes on
the runway.

They tell me I can land.

The wheels unfold.

# Welcome to New York

The plane lands at about 240 kilometres per hour.

We are in New York!

It was a good flight and everyone is happy.

# Glossary

**air-traffic control**
They control all the planes in the sky and at airports.

**captain**
The pilot in charge of the plane and its crew.

## co-pilot

The co-pilot helps the pilot to fly the plane.

## runway

A long, straight, smooth roadway used for take-offs and landings.

# Index

Copyright © ticktock Entertainment Ltd 2008
First published in Great Britain in 2008 by ticktock Media Ltd.,
Unit 2, Orchard Business Centre, North Farm Road, Tunbridge Wells, Kent TN2 3XF
ISBN 978 1 84696 765 8 pbk
Printed in China

We would like to thank: Penny Worms, Shirley Bickler, Suzanne Baker and the National Literacy Trust.

Picture credits (t=top, b=bottom, c=centre, l=left, r=right, OFC= outside front cover)
AirTeamImages (Tomas Coelho): 15. BAA Aviation Photo Library: 11. Cameron Bowerman: 20-21. Corbis: 4. The Flight Collection: 9, 10, 16, 17, 21t. Brian Futterman: 19. Daniel Hamer: 12. John Kelly: 6-7. Gary Lewis (ATCO Aviation photography): 13.

Every effort has been made to trace the copyright holders, and we apologise in advance for any unintentional omissions. We would be pleased to insert the appropriate acknowledgements in any subsequent edition of this publication.